ARRIVAL
SELECTED POEMS

DORAINE PORETZ

BOMBSHELTER PRESS

Other books by Doraine Poretz:
  Re:Visions
  This Woman In America
  Scattered Light

Some of these poems have appeared in the following magazines:
*ONTHEBUS, Bachy, Electrum, CQ, Harbinger, Poetry/LA, Dreamworks, LA
Free Press, California State Quarterly, Connections.*

My thanks to Ginette Mizraki for permisssion to use her artwork and to
Michael Andrews for the book design.

Library of Congress Catalog Number: 93-074960
ISBN 0-941017-37-0

BOMBSHELTER PRESS
1092 Loma Drive, Hermosa Beach, CA 90254

FOR MY MOTHER AND FATHER

CONTENTS

PART III. ANGELS

WITH GRATITUDE

MEETING IN SUMMER

I lean on a white, broken chair
by a broken, white window.
You fill my glass with Riesling as another light descends
catching a pair of bees.
Across the wide stone floor, a crooked trunk.
It houses knives, a strong collection
from all your trips into South American jungles.

Life, you tell me, is distance.
That and how to get to water by nightfall.

I run my hand along the smooth, cool wall.
You catch it, say: I love the heat. It forces me
to explain things to myself.
What have you learned? I ask.

That there is always water.
Somewhere. Waiting.

ARRIVAL

I.
LOVERS

MESSAGES

arrange white poppies in a vase
mornings into mornings the brown needling through

       words repeating like a bolt of cloth
       flipped out on a table the salesman
       saying you can cut it anywhere
       because of the pattern

a neighbor visits, a sculptor
who lugs five hundred pounds of rock
from the desert
i listen to the stone before i cut, she says
one wrong move
can shatter it

       you are capable of leaving the ground
       he tells me get rid of the baggage
       you mean verbiage i think to myself

a storm in new england
kills a whole village
i burst out crying
then wipe up the dishes

       * * *

this morning on this city corner
there is light from the country
the plants in my small room
sing with light, and the old woman
of my dream comes back

       come with me come it is not so difficult
       and the wide skirt swings from her hips
       and her neck skin shakes as she laughs

show me old woman
show me how to dance from room to room
not caring

that when i look back
i'm gone

***

to get used to being alive
is to kill your lovers
is to remember the navajos
who let one thread slip
in each of their otherwise
most perfect rugs

LONGING

It was all day, I say the longing was all day
It was all night, all night was the longing
And it swayed in my arms like a fragrant boy
And it cut through my heart like razored steel
And it sang, O it sang
like a shell undiscovered on a second moon
It was all day
It was all night
It was all
And is

       still

LISTEN, THIS BED:

it's the room.
The inside of a tooth, a china
cup. The Grand Canyon National Park you can take your clothes off.
Or you don't have to.
Listen, this kneecap?
It's the bed. And your knuckle my wrist you can leave your clothes on
if that's what you want, I'm taking my clothes off,
what will you do?

The night! The cracked sink! The cars like waves!

Of course your mouth,
these quarks, this laser
beam, this black hole,
no, don't stop,
your fingers taste—
don't laugh—
fuschia!
Of course,
laugh!
It's the Dance, the Right, the Trip
to deepest Africa. (Your eyes are wet.)

This bed.
The flashback of a flashback:
nettles beneath trees in woods behind your house all right stop.
If you want. I will too.
Look. And be quiet. I will be quiet too.

The space between the fingers of this hand
when the fingers are opened
or in a fist,
the same space exists.
In the same instant.
In us.
In this bed.

Begin.

IMMERSION

i watch her bathe
she fills the cup with water
i am the cup
i am the water
the wind outside flips leaves
they fill the night

i rub her back, her legs
the towel kisses her
warm her chest and small vagina
warm my mouth on her neck
i take her to the window
and when my shirt swings open
she touches my breast
i shiver my daughter i suckle you

she quivers rubbed rose
she shines
my face in her hair
it is fine to be tucked beside her
curled as a bean sprout unfolding
my dreams have arms

i reach under the covers
and feel her toes
perfect
in my hand

LOVE POEM

Last night: voluptuous.
Did you feel it too?
A black goblet filled with still, rich port.
I had been away, confused.
But last night
I came back.
I watched you listening to music;
the room was semi-dark,
lit by one, red, polished lamp.
When you looked up at me,
I recognized myself.
What are we to each other?
I think
different facets
of the same gem.
Turning, turning
in the hand of God.

THE EXCHANGE
for Vaslaw Nijinsky

Nijinsky!
        That splendid rose
                leapt

through the casement
woke the sleeping girl

Later, he was carted off to a cell

        (A man soars only to suffocate
        in what he can't contain.)

And the girl?
She witnessed what price miracle

        (Her eyes remain the dream in his head...)

END OF AN AFFAIR

I.
I have bitten him for blood;
he has ripped up 100 dollar books.
We like
to clarify
our feelings.
We've taken to writing poetry to each other.
I have stacks of his poems, and whenever I don't know
what he is talking about, I look it up
in his poetry.
By the time I've understood,
he's gone.

II.
We draw pictures for the small girl with green eyes.
This is a house, I say. The small green-eyed girl
points to a tree and teases: This is a house.
Well, it is, he says, for squirrels and birds.
But it's really a tree.
What is a tree, really? she asks.

III.
Making love to me he becomes a bear
or disappears into a wing of a boy.
I misinterpret longing, call it love.
At the very sweetest moment,
I turn it inside out, imagining him gone.

He has seen me hide under tables.
I have known him too terrified to leave his own apartment.
This exchange becomes mathematical
when we sit discussing blame
in a cold kitchen.

VI.
He says he is committed to me as if I were some asylum.

VII.
He has a key to my apartment. The light is on in the bathroom.
He comes in and takes off his clothes and gets into bed.
I have a key to my apartment. The light is on in the bathroom.
I come in and take off my clothes and get into bed. He turns over
and gets out of bed. The light is still on in the bathroom. And
I get out of bed and turn it off, and he is back, in bed, rolling
from his belly onto his back when I get into bed on the furthest side,
close to the wall.
He pretends he is sleeping.
He tells me later
I sleep with my mouth open.

A BRACELET OF HAIR

for my daughter

I.

Home to night and to you
swerved on the old satin quilt, your witch puppet
spread-eagled on the bed, mouth open.
Whatever is photographed curls,
the house alive with dead smells: a clump of old carnations.

I drop my clothes like skin,
(like a snake? you asked yesterday)
and turn the hall light off
and turn the bathroom light off
and run hot water in the tub
slip in like an egg to be poached.

Floating in dark the tilted moon rocks. Empty.

Night seeps in; you grind your teeth.
Perhaps you already know the way we love will disappear.

II.

The sun streams in, crayon rays between the poinsettias.
You snore. What wonderful noises! You small creature,
you lovely animal! And I think for a moment there is possibility;
that we might move like animals,
circling each other without longing,
and death would come easy as seasons—
but no—
minutes later, my coffee rests thick in the cup.
You chomp cornflakes, quiz me about the length of bees.
The day forces description.

III.

I drop you off (like skin?)
behind the metal fence
with all the eager children.
Your lunch pail bangs like a boat.
A stranger draws you in,
her arm around your shoulder.
And you arch your neck,
looking back.

LOOKING AT YOU WHILE YOU SLEEP

The bed is large,
and now hours after making love,
you are tucked on one side of it,
a continent away.
Nude as a boy, your lips quiver,
intaking breath; your chest
my two palms side by side
grown large by so much loving.

I wonder if there are mountains of snow in your dreams.
I think of snow because the moon has lit up the sheets.
Your hands are marvelous, whole. Graced without reason
by your side. And your head, sunk into the pillow:
some meteor fallen to earth,
some broken star.

LIVING TOGETHER

He wants me to see
all the horror films with him.
5 in a row through the midnight show until 4 a.m.
To point out effects:
Dracula's teeth inserted in shy girls' necks,
how the camera catches his stare,
the lightning, the lighting,
the shadow thrown when the French doors fly open,
and Linda in silk, her platinum bob on the pillow,
closes her eyes...
How the line: "It is better, after all, to be frightened
than to be crushed", is poetry.
Bela Lugosi—
how he died an addict believing himself Dracula—
is poetry.

He wants to catch the Festival of Frankenstein
with Basil Rathbone to compare it
with Andy Warhol's interpretation.

He wants
to share
adrenaline.

He wants to see all
the horror films,starting with the ones made in 1929,
to trace the evolution of monster
so that we can appreciate horror
together.

I tell him
loving him
is terrifying
enough.

ELEGY

Dear James,

Once you mentioned The Lie,
and I didn't understand
you were giving me the key to the treasure,
the one who is The Other,
the Opened Flower.

These many months I have come face to face:
standing inside the mirror looking out
standing outside the mirror looking in
until finally
I am just
standing.

When I thought I had love, I had none.
When I thought I had no love, I had none.
When I thought love was only for them,
I had no one.
Now, I simply have it,
and it's no longer mine.

We can't talk to each other the way we used to.
What I miss most is your beautiful, impish face.
As for words, they mean less and less.
Before there was such a lust for explanations, for definitions.
What music would we be now?

And you? How is it without your body? Having discarded
the ultimate definition.
You told me I would have to "receive".
The news of your death was hard,
but that too is now mine.

Perhaps, I'll be blessed with a dream,
you speaking in my inner ear.
But the words would not be words;
instead tears, a fragrant laughter, an inhalation of breath
before prayer.

For now, the poem
is the closest thing to grace I know.
As I cannot hold you anymore,
or let you go.

NO DISTANCE

not night
but black
like the night
after hot winds
polish it, yet
not again
black
but a sheen
mica
or crow wings
singed by moonlight
no matter
i sleep in the oregon woods
and you a hundred miles south
i enter
my breath
moves
that frond
outside your door
there! did you think that shift
is climate? something else to gauge?
no, these ways surrounding
i choose to name
not air
but love
deep
longing

A POSSIBILITY

The man is large
with a beauty that shouldn't be allowed
because it breaks the eye
with its form.

The woman is large
with an eye that shouldn't be allowed
because it breaks the beauty
with its sight.

She is teaching him gesture: the shade of
yes as he looks at her mouth,
the emphasis
on the last syllable of her name.

He is teaching her stealth: to feed a coyote
five feet
from their door.

On a deck in the canyon,
the man watches a hummingbird.
The woman listens to Rachmaninoff.

Together they eat cool pears
from a blue enamel bowl.

THIS WOMAN IN AMERICA
for Mary Ellen

Still she reads about the war.
Slender boys behind the bamboo.
Veterans playing poker in wheelchairs.

She often dreams the same movie:
the hero in a deserted room, looking for the scene of the crime,
wind blowing the open curtains. He flushes tissues down the toilet,
and the plumbing breaks.
Severed arms and legs rise up,

rise like his body in the early morning,
when he held her in the dark; the times
when even the sheets are afraid.

Lately she tells her son many things about the body.
What a magical machine it is.
They spend hours fitting a plastic skeleton,
figuring out directions.
He asks for more glue.
He asks for red to paint the heart.
He asks her to point out
the wishbone.
He wants to know if when we die
does the body disappear?
And if it does,
is it crying on the way down?

THE GIFT

for Andrew Wyeth

This is what the painter saw
and what he wanted more
than anything:
to light a thing into more than what was seen.
That blue stuffed couch, that porcelain vase?
They are nothing
until they are believed.
That woman's face asleep?
Now, it's Song.

Yet looking
at this painting
is listening
not
to music,

but what makes music
happen.

NOW

The morning light
sails through the window
breaking the glass like straight vodka
An earthquake in Armenia
kills fifty thousand
This morning continues

gathering within corners of rooms
dust and more dust
uncovering another arm, another torso
while you disappear into the pick-up

A shaft of light broadens
illuminating white, tiny particles
a weird confetti
celebrating, I trust, some victory
I watch it pour forth
so much light
so much dust
streaming

The motor fades
You are probably to the end of the road by now
When you return it will be dark
We will climb to bed
a few feet from a ceiling
which could fall any moment into our arms:
Earth has such desire!

And I,
rapt by longing,
have wasted so much

THE TURNING

Waking this morning, I miss
my daughter's drinkable limbs,
the simmering water of her eye.
She is growing up, a shadow now
in the whiteness of my rivered arms,
disappearing
as the sun shifts the hemispheres
of her body, soul, and mind.

The sun rising, rises within her another terrain,
setting her apparently further away.
She is fainting
out of childhood,
into the loveliness of woman,
and I am proud she has an imagining of that woman—
more than I did at her age.

I offer smelling salts,
a strong assurance she is splendid,
that her tiny breasts, her sweet fertility
do not mark her less
than her mind and heart would know.
For her, no gagged utterances:
music flows in her narrow frame,
bearing a female blessedness.

Just now I see her. Picking up one stone, and now another,
raising each to her ear,
listening...

PHOENIX

This prehistoric thing,
this "love"
is not shaped in a heart of a syllable.
Words parade, blind *Dummkopfs*,
while this black lump smolders,
waiting for the blue heat to facet the brilliance
of what it must become.

When does the poet
finally walk forward—
hands released like birds—
embracing all who have so patiently waited
these many thousands of years?
The only worthwhile translations
are in
what terrifies most.
Then faith
takes hold.

Kiss the circle of my grief, why don't you?
Suck in the sweetness that radiates in spite of everything.
Just don't ask me to explain,
for I trust nothing named.

I wait to receive the Other;
the one who is my heir and benefactor.
I wait for her to return.
This time without
the mockery of nouns, the past tense of verbs.

A fire in the belly stays coiled.
Wings whir.
True desire
takes time.

FINALLY

Sitting first, now leaning against
a tapioca-colored wall.
A drink steadies your hand.
It is a long distance from this side of the room.
As I walk,
I find your face, as usual,
not easy to find.
I am about to explain, then stop.
Haven't you remembered anything?
I touch your sleeve, and when you pull away
I am not offended. (Finally, no one is watching.
Or shall I say, finally, I have nothing to hide.)

And when I turn, it is just the way
I turned so long ago
when my heart wasn't sure
it could stand so much bliss.
But it did.
And it will.

SONG

You have been my occasion for grief,
I am grateful.
You have pulled me into the body of Mother,
I am re-membered.
You of the vulnerable eye,
of the frightened hand
and unutterable heart,
I made you what you were
as always
we make the other
into what we are to know about ourselves.

Through this time I dream what you cannot permit your body.
What I finally permit my own:

> The moon-struck girl stays curled in the womb
> of the Goddess; the Old Crone stares...

Whatever was most denied,
this grief has given.
Whatever most alone

hears.

PRAISE

Nights
and the stars rain down,
tiny shafts of mica
in the mine of these hills.
Each plane of our skin lit,
and we appear,
finally, what we are.

In the wooden kitchen, a ballet of pears.
A young woman stirs soup, and the steam rises.
It is praise enough,
the vegetables which have scooted underground,
dark tubers to be pulled.
It is praise,
the way we have come together.

Days we go out our separate doors,
circling back to the wood.
In May it is simple enough to make love to trees
as to ourselves.
We imagine ribbons, a pole.
The trees too have their circle;
their limbs stretch up
holding streamers.

Once our bodies felt strange,
baggage strapped to our bones.
Now they slide like water down our mouths.
In the pelt of such lunacy, believing ourselves gods,
the bear of our nightmare
transforms. We are

a family in this world.
Underground too long, we did not understand
that spring is a matter of letting be.
It is simple then,
nothing more

than the slow moment
from snow to water
from water to wind
to fire
to praise.

THE MARRIAGE

He was sent away to war and returned in war,
blood on his thighs. She rubbed her body down
until the bones shone white.
But this too is you, he cried.
She turned her head away.

Every night he found her
staring through the dark, waiting for the deer
to come from the hills. He recoiled, pulled
the sheet across his eyes, heard her whisper:
This too is you.

And the years passed, each one a threat,
banging down the door,
hiding faceless in the shrubs,
until there was nothing to protect,
nowhere to go, except, through each other
and to themselves.

And the dream broke. And spilled across them like moonlight.

The husband turned over, remembering what was his,
pulled the woman toward him as the sky flapped from his chest,
letting his woman out. And the woman ended her mourning
as her body's seas convulsed,
thrusting out the man in her
as she pulled her husband in.
And all four embraced,
for what seemed like forever.
Not having done so in O
too long
a time.

FOR THE POEM

This week I stay alive
by reading the last poem I've written
over and over again.
I take my poem into evening light
and let it sing
against concrete. I walk into the house,
set it down under an ashtray, the thin slip of paper flapping,
resisting a breeze from the window. Then,

I wash the dishes from the night before.
The doorbell rings.
It's the pharmacy with medicine for my daughter.
She doesn't want the medicine. It spills on the sheets,
the sheets I washed an hour before. Finally,
she is sleeping in my bed,
and before I tear up her bed,
I read my poem again and think:
Christ, it's a beautiful poem.

Now, I'm in her room,
tripping over dolls, cursing all the dust,
wishing I had a club so I could club them all to death.
In the kitchen now, tearing pumpernickel off a loaf,
eating it without butter, only because I am out of butter,
folding my poem, smoothing down the white square of it,
when suddenly,
the telephone rings.

It is Stephen, the man I'm sleeping with and love,
telling me it's all been a mistake from the beginning,
and hanging up the phone, like in a dream and dreaming still,
I feel the poem in my hand,
and I unfold it, slowly, delighting how the creases flatten out,
how the ink stays dry, in spite of itself,
and I read it again, aloud (this time softly),
and I laugh, I laugh!

Grateful,
everything's
possible.

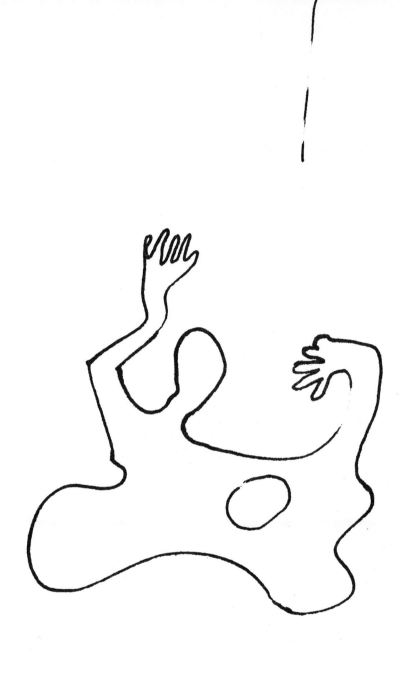

II.
STRANGERS

SAMUEL SPEAKS

...we shall love, we shall
hate, but it will be like music,
sheer utterance, issuing straight
out of the unknown.

—D.H. Lawrence

Twelve breakdowns have had me.
One for each apostle.
The first movement one hundred and twenty times
this week alone. It saves me. Beethoven understands tone
as planets. (Hooves. Rose crystal. Constellations through bone.)
My heart. My brain. They were crowned once, you know.
In gold. And my mouth. Throat. The way I shoulder you
in this small room. You move away. All instruments warp.
No chance to go completely mad in joy.
(It is the feat of modern medicine that I speak to you at all.
A gift. The not. The no-tone of careful departures and returns.)

Did you know that death plays the bones for razored music?
Well, it's not a pretty song.
But I might heal myself forever in the desert,
where ocotilla strapped to light cry out I could go alone
and chant or whirl my patterns,
and any wind could wind me up and fling me out:
a top
spinning toward heaven.

And you would be there to welcome me. After.
For who are we to each other if not a mirror?
To witness joy and terror,
to diagram horizons?

I CAN DESTROY THE CHILDREN

so quietly
that even the neighbors wouldn't know,
so quietly
that even my best friend who comes every afternoon for coffee
wouldn't know
I ingest whole bodies.

When the clock mocks the growth
of that fat palm outside my window,
I am
their country.
When I make war, they are drafted. And I own
all the machines.
And when I hate,
their thin ears and eyes
are orifices of desire.

Fact: These are my children. What does that mean?

At one moment lover, I swoop them up.
They reject me. They'll pay.
The perfect incision of my eye
until finally they recede
to their rooms, tearing paper.

At night, I hear them talking in their sleep.
When I get to their door to listen, they stop.
The Santa Anna winds have come on;
they slaughter the leaves with such grace!

I go back to bed but can't sleep,
tracing what is real in me
to the elements.

THIS WOMAN IN AMERICA
for Lyla

In the morning
she sometimes dances
to the music on the radio,
the FM plugged into the kitchen, the rayon housecoat
slipping
off her shoulder.
Or walks around the house naked,
cleaning toilet bowls with Ajax.
Sunk into formica, she smokes tiny brown cigarettes
as she completes her mail order telephoning.
Dog hairs stick to the coffee cup,
(She kicked the mutt hard last week because he kept nosing
her crotch), and her son
is talking in sign language.
Once a beautiful baby, now he smells of sweat,
stones birds, brings home
sly notes in his lunch box.

After she left her husband, her life began.
She stopped biting her cuticles
and her therapist canceled her.
But now, getting up in the morning,
without that fearful weight beside her,
sprawled like an angry root, sucking her in,
she pulls the sheets up clear around her shoulders,
no longer knowing
what it is
which keeps her.

PHOTOGRAPH

The old people
have lived for forty-five years
on Fairfax Avenue.
They spend their time
placing small amounts of food
left over in large plastic containers
into small plastic containers.
They spend their time
placing sweet Concord wine
left over in large glass bottles
into small plastic ones.
They spend their time
placing small amounts of
words
left over in large
memories
into small containers of misery
so that their time
formed
in old age
becomes the space
of quiet
in
their
mouths.

FROM HIS CHILDHOOD

my favorite supper is mashed potatoes and butter. daddy finishes
fast. he fixes the fan. he sweats a lot and smells. agatha is
my sister and she's two and eats potatoes raw or off the floor
when she doesn't get smacked for doing it. mommy never eats.
she stays in the bathroom and puts black circles under her eyes.
tonight the moon outside my window looks like a banana, i would like
to swing from it, to swing and daddy says clean your plate goddammit!
uncle michael takes me to the aquarium. i put my ear to the glass,
it feels cold and sad and uncle michael says what you doin' that for,
boy? the fish knock into each other without doors and plates and
goddammits and going to sleep i bunch up the sheets and they wrinkle
like the waves and mommy comes into my ocean with her red fish mouth,
kisses me, the light under the door so thin, he could never pull
her out. even with his long rope.(i smell her skin.)
she is going out with him, with wet potatoes on his breath
and pearls around her neck. she is too beautiful to love me.
his arm all hairy around her white, white neck.

THIS WOMAN IN AMERICA
for Kate

I have to climb through the window;
she has given me the wrong key.
She tells me later that lovers
must find their way to each other.
(Her teeth are yellow leaves)
She takes her art seriously,
spoons up coke to clear her head
and writes into the dark.
She holds my head and tells me I'm an ugly boy,
bug-eyed and thick lipped, then kisses my mouth and chest
then shakes me off
like snow.
My dreams, she says, all motorcycle past,
like all the men I've known.

The room is white with pages
rising from the floor.
I help her stack chapters. With each one done,
she takes off
another piece of clothing.
There are 22 chapters to go:
I'll wait to see bone.

Later that night, this time the windows nailed shut.
Through the vent, she yells.
On the bed we lie among the mess of white paper.
The room is fluorescent. White.
I can't keep secrets, she says, but I forget what I know.
It's enough to wash this flesh!

She slaps her shy belly
and rubs her hair
and stretches her arms lengthwise on the pillows:
Tack me up on the wall, next to the clippings of all
my young and famous novelists. Push in hard.

AMERICAN LANDSCAPE

You see him crossing Wilshire and Galey
3 filthy blankets under his arm. Near MOMA, 52nd and 5th
and later on the steps of St. Patrick's, flying with pigeons.
In a doorway in Albuquerque, pulling at a flabby arm, fingers
bitten pencils writing home to that sidewalk down the block,
terrified, a little drunk, thumbing a ride on a 2 dollar tortilla
and cheese, he can't be more than 19.
You rummage through your purse not looking telling yourself
this is how to behave, so as not to make him ashamed.
Watching her at the supermarket in Vegas next to the porkchop
special your brown paper bags too heavy to lift
not as heavy as a dead body though.
In the bus in Atlanta, close enough to trace the lattice work
on his bulbous nose this is the closest you've ever been
to any of them. Hanging in the trees in New Orleans
leaning against a metal fence in Chicago. In Hackensack
you're driving down the street and see a sign: "i need a room"
You circle back 3 blocks and tell your kid to give the man 5 bucks.
She comes back, says: "He blesses us and tells us Jesus saves."
You look away ashamed.

You're home.
You're tired from work and traffic. From a career that never came.
They are all waiting for you at the door.
You hear your dead father telling you how 10 of them
got a tablespoon of meat a month, but that was in Russia,
long before you were born.
You invite them in. It's hard to sleep. You feel safer with them.
(They have a way with the dark, you explain to yourself.)
They pile their Bibles, stack their yo-yos, balls of string,
forks, broken plates, buttons, rhinestone rings, Inquirer and LIFE
magazines, porcelain salt and pepper dog and cat shakers, watches,
empty or half-filled bottles of scotch and shampoo
and take turns
singing you to sleep.

In the dream, the children cough up blood sausages.
You run to get them water; they're so grateful
their little hearts melt
into one, gigantic disfigurement. And when you try
to pull their hearts apart,
each child starts screaming. But you insist:

No, no, each of you deserves
his or her own, very own heart.
But they keep screaming...

You wake. Your nightgown soaked, hiked above your knees.
It's cold. You're exposed. And they're gone.

You pad into the kitchen.
The ants are drowning in a dump of sugar.
Your six-year-old coughs in the next room.
You go in and put the cover back over her trembling body,
then sit in the kitchen again, burning a blue light
while the conflagration rages
on the other side
of the black glass.
You sit for a long, long while; but nothing changes.
And you are startled by your thin humanity,
humbled by the breadth of your loss.

Your breathing comes on fast.

THIS WOMAN IN AMERICA

for Lily

1.
tea in the red china pot
one hand closed on a cup
the other pulled on the robe
pressing a skinny breast

> the cough from his room won't quit
> the cry from his room won't quit
> the whores getting theirs
> in the wells of the brownstones
> new york city a bed
> children curl down in cement

the kid in the bed won't quit
the cough, the cry
the cold
unlit tile, the blue
flame, the
red
china
pot

2.
She had been dreaming:
> her father was kissing
> her eyes...

3.
she tried to quiet the child
when she had to, had to, he kept
at it, wouldn't stop it,
wouldn't stop,
her hand through his sweet pink mouth
her fingers like birds taking off
breaking like eggs

hitting
his head
taking him
down
through feathers
through bed
through the
blue
flame
the
red
pot

THE DARK RIVER

So I put my hand out further,
a little further, and I felt that
which was not I.

—D.H. Lawrence

He has the bones of a boy.
When I hold him,
my arms insinuate like thread,
sewing a perfect pocket of desire.
There are secrets even in the way he eats a chip,
biting it delicately between his front teeth;
in the way he holds his cigarette,
the burning end toward him.

All night we sit in candlelight and talk of Poland.
The train between Paris and Warsaw
has nothing to do with romance:
loot stashed in compartments,
five years if caught smuggling a press.

What is it like to read a book and be afraid?
To watch your house burn?
He smiles, bites slyly
on another chip. (How can I begin...)
breaks it (...to understand?) sweetly.

Suddenly,
he pulls me toward him,
fitting my head to his chest.
Suddenly,
I am a girl:
innocent, just now,
for the first time, for
the first time,
ever.

THE MOTHER HARBORS RED

A flamenco dancer's dream when young,
the Mother harbors red. Summer, summer still,
but heat unlike a thunderstorm or drought.
A threat of red
in aggravated shouts; the deft scrape of knife
against the beet.
The Mother harbors red
between her thighs, which open to nights and novels;
while her husband sleeps like a kidney.

The Mother makes the bed.
A rash of light between the blinds
distorts her fragrant skin. She cuts thread with her teeth.
The others insist
her lips grow thin.

The last child leaves.
The Mother's face miraculously smooth
for 64 years
suddenly grows branches.

She laughs outloud,
spends the remaining months
playing mahjong
cooking
thick
stews.

THIS WOMAN IN AMERICA
for Edith

My son
ripped me up like crabgrass.
We're going home, he said, back to New York.
You're old, Ma, and with me gone, there's no one.

The car was packed.
He had no room for one brown box
of glass clowns and carnival dolls.
Junk, he said, you're always collectin' junk.
A neighbor said she'd repack the car, and he got mad:
Don't need no one to tell me how to pack a car.

The trip, how hot it was, the sweat drippin' down
like grease off a cooked duck.
We share a three room apartment.
Makes him proud to think the others think
he took me in.
I live like a border though I pay a quarter of the rent.
He plans to get a rocker, shuts
the livin' room door when he has a girl.
I hear them whisperin' and laughin' in the hall.
What am I supposed to do? Walk around the bed?

He's killin' me in good conscience.

He tells me any other old woman
would be happy resting, livin' in a fine place.
I raised two kids in the Depression, worked 50 years straight through,
I'm not the smartest woman in this world.
But I'm not
any other
woman.

I'll turn the oven on first, and give him that
for an inheritance.
I will, I tell you.
I will.

OBSESSION

you big black cat with tourmaline eyes
you trample my garden and cry for milk
and like a fool I feed you
secrets are in your fur
they whisper in pink and wet tongues
and your breath smells of half-eaten birds
a sparrow wing sticks from your mouth
I will not let you in my house

I still wear the ring with your eye set in it
I am a queen with such a ring of tourmaline and diamonds
and forget that your face lies waiting to spring
in the tangle of veins
in my hand you big cat

once you were gray with white markings
and I played with you on my bed
you purred and kneaded at my breast
I practically nursed you
when you died in the basement
I smelled you for days
I buried you between brick and ended it

now, you animal, you're back in your new night robe
with one eye closed like a wound
scratching at the window
breathing on glass
if I beat you on the head with a stick
or mangle you under tires
I will never be rid of you

I open the cupboard
hairs fly up in my mouth
you have slipped in the house
through the floorboards
I smell your spray in the hall
one small paw
spreads
beneath my bedroom
door

IN THE EIGHTH HOUSE

You grew up more brilliant than the rest
amidst beige stretching the prairie,
a sure braid of wheat 'round the heart,
your heart
a bundle of wild
flowers. Strangers trickled in,
teasing brush in need of streams,
turning to look at tractors
the moment you were spinning
toward the stars.

At ten you held stones in your mouth to stop a stutter—
the flap of wild geese from your tongue—
betrayed by the counsel that what is heard
is uttered,
and not the silence inbetween.

Believing in hell, you pretended to feel less,
fearing ghosts would gather you,
catapult you out through shingle and brick
into the broad Nebraska night.

And now, years later—
in spite of the roads which have brought you back
to your first born,
in spite of the blood on each door
alerting death's angel to pass—
you lean in close, whispering:
"I cannot be counted on to keep in touch"
whispering
the prairie is vast and echoless
extending
for miles.

THIS WOMAN IN AMERICA
for Sylvia

No one forced us, Martin. We fell in love,
although there were
reservations on the part of our parents.
But we were ready. We were.

You told me it would be all or nothing,
through thick and thin, and I was impressed
with your loyalty. (Now, stop smiling, Martin. I'm serious.
I am not getting melodramatic.)

Lord knows some never find one
they can spend 25 years of their lives
and not dream of opening them up with forks.
I've never had any nightmares about you, Martin.
Not that I remember, that is.
So, it isn't that I'm ungrateful.
I've had more than most, I know.
It's just that once

I had something else in mind.
More (or maybe less) than
two children
and cat hairs between the seams of stretched out barbecues.
Not stardom, exactly. Although I spent the first two years like you,
lying in wait for the call;

no, all I mean is
today. I picked up our daughter at school,
and I watched the young girls embracing,
their clean and clear collar bones in the sun,
and I knew that I had something else in mind, once.
And it hurt.
And it still
hurts.

FOR THE CHILDREN OF THE LOST SONG

...but trailing clouds of glory
do we come from God who is our
home...

—William Wordsworth

The Drivers were ready
when the sun was sex,
lavender and red between the hills.
It smoked, glowed, then disappeared
and we were rounded out of Song
and the Night quickly ours.
Thick redundant Night, we passed through,
crouched in our seats
unutterable in our longing.

The Drivers passed back fudge
when we were good. (So be good be good be good).
Nights on the road, our eyes wide, we pretended to sleep.
And the monster trucks had monster eyes.
And the monster trucks carried unnamables, strapped beneath canvas,
(so be good be good be good).

And the Drivers absolute!
And the Road absolute!
And the Night, O, the Night!

And it seemed like years...

It was not the uncertainty of death; oh,
we knew that would come. But rather,
the smile through the bruise,
and never touching us, the gaze.
And finally the dust in our mouths, the shadows around our wrists,
insured we would never know to touch ourselves,
or anyone else.

And indeed, it was years...

At last, morning came.
But not a morning of gulls. Or slivered light between.
Rather a name for not-night, an ocher phosphorescence.

Bereft, no child moved; until one
then another rose (Why, no one knew),
pulled up by something, some sweetness
issuing from the radiant darkness.
Such sweetness once, just once!

And so,
at any moment,

again.

III.
ANGELS

THE BIRTHING

Night embeds me with a spear of miracles.
Day pulls back to reveal its well.
Alone, stars surround me.
Alone, two angels hold my head.

What is forming has no measure.
What is re-membering has no design.
What is loving but surrendering:
Man/Woman: Mine.

A WAVE, A PARTICLE

You must lose your mind
to come to your senses.

—**Fritz Perls**

I.

I wake, startled into the middle of my life,
climb down the wooden slats from my loft,
a height I imagine flying from.
In the kitchen I cut an apple.
The white fruit is sweet, and when the meat disappears,
I am grateful.
The tiny seeds sleep snugly in their cores.
I usually throw them away, but this morning I plant them
next to three broken steps in the dark earth.
Perhaps a tree of lemons or pomegranates will rise.
The dark, I have learned, has its own laws.

> what am i to you if not
> a reaching toward, a pulling back?
> what am i to myself
> if not toward/back at once?
> i move to the music of atoms
> i appear to be one, but am more
> the dreamer the dreamed the dreaming

II.

Flat against the open air rise the hills, the trees, the sky.
In the midst of the mayhem and rape, they reside.
The hills circle the sun.
The trees stretch out their arms.
The sky still bares its beautiful chest to the moon.
And I feel foolish remembering one smoggy night,
crying out to them: Hold on!
As if to say that I with others of my kind will rescue you.
Tonight they turn to me, in their unerring calm,
sure within their fold, for whatever time
they have surrendered to.

It is not they
who are in danger.

III.

We must love one another or die, a poet said.
Was that a threat?
Grace lies
not just in heaven; here too.
How to make it true?

IV.

Repeat your words over and over
and laugh until your head rolls off, the Master said.
Everything you bear, you bring to bear in words.
But it is the rest—
that which is unbearable—

which is love.

THE LESSON

The woman who needed to explain everything
went down to the stream as the old woman
had instructed her to do.
She picked out the stones, one by one.
(How she knew which ones to choose, I do not know.
It had something to do with feeling, I suppose.)

Pulling each from the cool, dark mud,
she wondered, why stones?
Stones are famine, mute.
She remembered walking barefoot on them,
how they pressed too deeply into her skin,
putting her off balance,
while they remained perfectly steadfast.
They are your gifts, the old woman had said.
Go to the river and dig for them.

And so she had, and placed them now
in a crooked row on the river's edge
and sat looking at them as they rested, silent,
in the sun.
There they were, apparently small, making no show.
Impeccably weighted and formed.
They asked for nothing, they knew enough.
She noticed how they shone.
(The sun having lit up their water-stained surfaces.)

And as she looked, all become one, polished movement of stone:
self-evident, good.

And finally,
she understood.

JOURNEY

In the beginning, the tree was far;
the trunk thick and dark, lit from behind on a hill.
The branches were heavy, leafless. Some almost touching
the earth. But not quite.

The tree haunted the ground, and from where she stood,
looking up at it, she could feel the tree trolls
turning beneath her. Awed, she came every sunset,
satisfied to gaze at a distance.

And then one evening, quite suddenly,
the tree was mantled in white blossoms.
Also, the tree had moved, or the earth had leveled.
She was forced to stand and stare so closely,
the blossoms became her sky.

Finally, there was no room, but the tree's room.
The trunk had grown so round, the branches spread like hawks,
if she were to remain, she had no other choice,
but to move inside.

                And terrified, she did.
                And amazed herself.

At once her body stretched to fire,
her face flew off like a dove's,
and her arms: a parenthesis of light.

Now, her darkness is the tree's darkness,
and her passion is from the root;
and her heart,
not shared,
but owned.

IN THIS COUNTRY

A ring of stars falls broken down the side of a building
Still the light is beautiful
Still it can be raised and worn
Inside a sudden flash of heaven
The Other enters
And what seemed interminable isolation
becomes desire and light and shapes itself
into an apple, a rose, a muscular leg
dancing toward itself

Your wonder now
is a country
White light loosens itself from a black-lit lake
God patiently fills
The great Leonardo said, *He turns not back who is bound to a star*

Now that you accept there is no end
What is the boon to offer up
and what the destination?

Only that you are dead no more
Only that you live
in this
country

THE VISIT

These days hold the flower
of all the flowers of the world.

Real Nature has come into my house.

She sits inside my living room, rocking.
All day, all night. Laughing.

JOGGING THROUGH

Flat stretch, I begin slow,
keep the pace when suddenly
everything takes shape: my breasts twin rubber balls,
the muscles in my legs, triangular homes poster-painted
against the hills.

I run I glide I gully the wind
My face whistles through my mouth
I am old with no teeth I am young
I am strung together, lashed by thin green scallions
which inch along the road
I am running I am flying I am thinking this is lovely
I am out of breath and smiling
I am out of breath and dying
Short, breaths, leave my mouth
One more yard
I will surely leave ground!

Cars stop.
Dogs screech their warning.
And the hills give up their escort.
(I am rounded again
as the water bead
balanced
on a
single
leaf.)

My house door gapes, more out of breath than I.
I sit on the stoop next to numbers which mark me in this field;
give up my sweat, my air, my red face to the birds.
Then I check my watch.
I have made better time than the day before:
each day
getting closer
to my
birth.

THE WORDING

In a world of slanted light

a man standing in the deep woods

on a patch of dried leaves

becomes a fawn His body is lithe His dark eyes tender

This then is love a mysterious greening

Why do I keep telling you this over and over?

Because I do not tell it

It is the same round of voices

Remind yourself of what you truly know

This wording then is action

A threading catching slanted lines

that purposely spell nothing

No other choice now but to see

No other choice then but to speak

No other choice

For death is just another kind of wording

Watching

In a series of silent syllables

In another forest

In another clearing

IN THE DESERT NIGHT
for Daniele

For you are the wishbone that shall stay whole.
A teepee of wonder, an Indian's promise.
An arrow of moons has startled your bones.
And no storms
Shall harm you.

Rise on your left foot, my slim-hipped darling.
Or rise on your right; you cannot fail.
For you are the lizard eating the sky.
Even as you are the mountain basking in sand.

And that is why desert animals prowling the night
Sleep peacefully by your side.

PHOENIX (2)

The door is open wide
letting in the other world.
You guess it was the night wind; you guess this
rather than admit some careless gesture.

You find something dark
on the smooth pine floor, and bending see
more closely: a hummingbird, apparently dead.
You whisper, Wake, please wake,
but it is still. And stiller the more you stare.
You dare not touch it, this holy mask, this cup
of vulnerability.

Just yesterday it was one of many,
shimmering like opals, dousing for sugared water,
its vibrancy catching the mountains in your throat.
Surrendering to death, you turn to get a cloth,
when suddenly

a geyser
a perpendicular thrust toward some other idea
makes you gasp.
The hummingbird beams, drops, rises again, tucking, pleating
the air, an accordion of delight
taking your breath out of itself.

You open every window, cajoling it, pointing to the nearest escape.
You even bring the hummingbird feeder in,
tempting it as if it were a cat!

The bird lands, resting on a sill.
By now you are sure it will suffocate or grow deranged
from the alien atmosphere of metal and glass.

Aflight again, this time toward your loft.
It circles, vibrates like a tuning fork,
then finally falls
into a nest of milkwhite pillows.

A hummingbird in your bed! A hummingbird alive where you dream!

It waits. You watch.
Finally you give in and climb up,
one foot gingerly on top of the other, pushing each rung
of the ladder down,
as you, rising higher,
meet it.

CONVICTION

I is another.
— **Rimbaud**

The bed is breathing, I said.
It's the wind, he said.

When I look at Durer's drawings of pillows
I see faces.
That's art, he says.

Early this morning,
I tiptoed into my child's room
and pushed the cover over her sleeping body.
Still dreaming, she mumbled:
I love you.

I believed her.

TO RIDE

a two wheeler
trusting
the Circle/the weight of our bodies
all
we're allowed.
(The balance seals the ride makes us birds/once more
my head between your hands)
          Years before

a mother or father
held the seat, steadied it, then disappeared,
and off we'd go,
down the grass slope in gales.
After the fall, we knew victory. Now,
it is not so clean: this moment to moment precariousness:
In childhood you learn something once, then grow up
          To love

without fear/the wheels taking off
so that nothing
before
holds anything out
but cellars
          To love

without dread/one hand off
the handlebars, then suddenly
no hands at all,

and all of the hills
turn to stars

THE RETURN

Because you look into their eyes
and see them turn their eyes away,
because they are afraid
to touch you.
Because for generation after generation
you have called each other lover, kin
yet still this,
and because of this,

you go out
breathless
to the hills.
You stare at the stars,
ride up to each of them;
and they take you, O yes, they take you,
hoisting you up by your armpits,
pressing you close to the wild night.

A hawk comes, circling an inscription, dedicating himself.
He circles slowly, knowing how hard it is
for one of your kind
to accept pure generosity.
A deer, his ears alert as any lover's body, looks straight at you,
and you are startled to see yourself in his gaze.
Slowly a smile, unbidden, spreads
reaching beyond the contours of your face,
weaving into the aroma of trees;
and you murmur: I am loved. And a moment later: I love.

And you who for hours, days, years before
were driven down,
scattered like ash by fears of all who curse the dark
and any kind of mystery, who put you out...out!
You speak the ineffable password now,
letting yourself in
to the only
real world.

At first you do not want to return to the house,
frozen on the side of the road.
But finally, you do. For they are waiting.
And you, you have something
to say.

ARRIVAL

Nightfall
The sky glutted with clouds
voluptuous with rain
A delicate lacework of leaves
is black against
a turquoise sky
So much joy
in one tree stretching its limbs!
So much forgiveness
in one walking past!
So thin the moon, an iridescent wafer
torn in half—
accessible patient
Without recrimination
it has taken me
this
long

DORAINE PORETZ

is a poet/playwright who works as a poet/teacher in various elementary and high schools in Los Angeles and Beverly Hills. She has served on the faculty of the California Summer School of the Arts and taught poetry workshops at the women's prison in Chino as part of UCLA's Artsreach program. Presently she teaches classes at the Beverly Hills Adult School in prose and poetry and offers a monthly writing seminar entitled, *Writing Down The Music Of Your Life*. This is her fourth book of poetry from Bombshelter Press.